Old Fashioned, Homemade Fudge Recipes

Only Authentic and Mouthwatering Fudge Recipes

By

Angel Burns

© 2019 Angel Burns, All Rights Reserved.

License Notices

This book or parts thereof might not be reproduced in any format for personal or commercial use without the written permission of the author. Possession and distribution of this book by any means without said permission is prohibited by law.

All content is for entertainment purposes and the author accepts no responsibility for any damages, commercially or personally, caused by following the content.

Get Your Daily Deals Here!

Free books on me! Subscribe now to receive free and discounted books directly to your email. This means you will always have choices of your next book from the comfort of your own home and a reminder email will pop up a few days beforehand, so you never miss out! Every day, free books will make their way into your inbox and all you need to do is choose what you want.

What could be better than that?

Fill out the box below to get started on this amazing offer and start receiving your daily deals right away!

https://angel-burns.gr8.com

Table of Contents

Mouthwatering Fudge Recipes 6

Recipe 1: Hot Chocolate Fudge 7

Recipe 2: Red Velvet Fudge.. 10

Recipe 3: Pumpkin Spice Pecan Fudge........................ 13

Recipe 4: Malt Fudge 15

Recipe 5: Mocha Almond Fudge 18

Recipe 6: Orange Creamsicle Fudge........................... 20

Recipe 7: Dark Chocolate Bourbon Fudge 22

Recipe 8: Key Lime Fudge... 25

Recipe 9: Cookie Butter Pecan Fudge......................... 28

Recipe 10: Mint Chocolate Chip Fudge...................... 30

Recipe 11: Rocky Road Fudge...................................... 33

Recipe 12: Snickerdoodle Fudge.................................. 36

Recipe 13: Gingerbread Fudge...................................... 39

Recipe 14: Peanut Butter Snickers Fudge 42

Recipe 15: German Chocolate Fudge............................ 44

Recipe 16: Cookie Monster Fudge................................ 47

Recipe 17: Sugar Cookie Fudge..................................... 49

Recipe 18: Root Beer Fudge 52

Recipe 19: Caramel Apple Fudge 55

Recipe 20: Cake Batter Fudge.. 57

Recipe 21: White Chocolate Peppermint Fudge 60

Recipe 22: Carrot Cake Fudge 62

Recipe 23: Hazelnut and Chocolate Pirouline Fudge.... 64

Recipe 24: Nutter Butter Fudge 67

Recipe 25: S'mores Fudge 70

About the Author 73

Author's Afterthoughts... 75

Mouthwatering Fudge Recipes

HHHHHHHHHHHHHHHHHHHHHHHHHHHHHHH

Recipe 1: Hot Chocolate Fudge

This is a delicious fudge recipe you can make to help bring two of your favorite winter desserts into one treat that is perfect to make whenever the winter begins to turn cold.

Yield: 12 servings

Preparation Time: 1 hour and 5 minutes

List of Ingredients:

- 2 cups of dark chocolate chips
- 1, 14 ounce can of sweetened condensed milk, evenly divided
- 1 ½ cup of white chocolate chips
- 1 ½ cups of miniature marshmallows

HHHHHHHHHHHHHHHHHHHHHHHHHHHHHHHH

Instructions:

1. In a bowl, add in the white chocolate chips and 5 tablespoons of condensed milk. Microwave for 30 seconds or until melted. Stir well until smooth in consistency.

2. In a separate bowl, add in the dark chocolate chips and remaining condensed milk. Microwave for 1 minute or until melted. Stir well until smooth in consistency.

3. Add a sheet of aluminum foil into a baking dish. Grease with cooking spray.

4. Spread the dark chocolate into the baking pan. Pour the white chocolate mix over the top.

5. Sprinkle the miniature marshmallows over the top.

6. Cover and place into the fridge to chill for 1 hour.

7. Slice and serve.

Recipe 2: Red Velvet Fudge

This is a decadent red velvet fudge dish that will impress your friends and family. Once you get a taste of it, you won't be able to stop at just one piece.

Yield: 16 servings

Preparation Time: 1 hour and 5 minutes

List of Ingredients:

- 3 cups of white sugar
- ¾ cup of butter
- 2/3 cup of half and half
- 1, 12-ounce bag of milk chocolate chips
- 1, 7-ounce jar of marshmallow crème
- 1 teaspoon of pure vanilla
- 1 cup of semi-sweet chocolate chips
- 1 ounce of red food coloring

HHHHHHHHHHHHHHHHHHHHHHHHHHHHHH

Instructions:

1. Add a sheet of aluminum foil into a baking dish. Grease with cooking spray.

2. In a bowl, add in the semi-sweet chocolate chips and red food coloring. Stir well to mix.

3. In a separate bowl, add in the butter. Microwave for 1 ½ minutes or until melted. Add in the white sugar and half and half. Stir well to mix. Microwave for 3 minutes. Stir again.

4. Add in the marshmallow crème, milk chocolate chips, pure vanilla and the food coloring mix. Stir well until smooth in consistency.

5. Pour into the baking dish.

6. Cover and place into the fridge to chill for 1 hour.

7. Slice and serve.

Recipe 3: Pumpkin Spice Pecan Fudge

This is the perfect fudge recipe to make just in time for the holiday season. While it made take a few minutes to prepare, it is a fudge recipe that can be made with ease.

Yield: 25 servings

Preparation Time: 15 minutes

List of Ingredients:

- 18 ounces of pumpkin spice morsels
- 1, 14 ounce can of sweetened condensed milk
- Dash of salt
- 1 teaspoon of pure vanilla
- 1 cup of pecans, roasted, chopped and evenly divided

HHHHHHHHHHHHHHHHHHHHHHHHHHHHHHHH

Instructions:

1. Place a sheet of aluminum foil into a baking dish. Grease with cooking spray.

2. In a saucepan set over medium heat, add in the pumpkin spice morsels, condensed milk and dash of salt. Cook for 2 minutes or until melted. Remove from heat.

3. Add in the pure vanilla and most of the pecans except for 3 tablespoons. Stir well to mix.

4. Pour into the baking dish.

5. Sprinkle the remaining pecans over the top.

6. Top and place into the fridge to chill for 2 hours or until firm.

7. Slice and serve.

Recipe 4: Malt Fudge

If you love the flavor of malt chocolate shakes, then this is one fudge recipe you need to make for yourself. Once you try it, you will want to make it as often as possible.

Yield: 64 servings

Preparation Time: 3 hours and 40 minutes

List of Ingredients:

- 3 cups of white sugar
- ¾ cup of butter, soft
- Dash of salt
- 1 cup of heavy whipping cream
- 11 ounces of white chocolate chips
- 7 ounces of marshmallow fluff
- ¼ cup of chocolate ovaltine
- 1, 12-ounce box of whoppers, chopped

HHHHHHHHHHHHHHHHHHHHHHHHHHHHHHH

Instructions:

1. In a baking dish, add a sheet of aluminum foil. Grease with cooking spray.

2. Add the chopped whoppers into a Ziploc bag. Seal the bag and smash until crushed. Set aside.

3. In a saucepan set over medium to high heat, add in the butter, white sugar, dash of salt and heavy whipping cream. Allow to come to a boil. Boil for 4 minutes. Remove from heat.

4. In a bowl, add in the white chocolate chips, chocolate ovaltine and marshmallow cream. Pour the butter mix over the top. Stir well until melted. Add in 1 ½ cups of crushed whoppers. Stir well to incorporate.

5. Pour into the baking dish. Top off with the remaining cup of crushed whoppers.

6. Cover and place into the fridge to chill for 3 hours.

7. Slice and serve.

Recipe 5: Mocha Almond Fudge

This is a fudge recipe that is so creamy and rich, you will want to spoil yourself with it as often as possible. It is so easy to make, you will want to make it as often as possible.

Yield: 8 servings

Preparation Time: 1 hour and 5 minutes

List of Ingredients:

- 1, 16-ounce pack of milk chocolate
- 1, 14 ounce can of sweetened condensed milk
- 1 ½ to 2 cups of cocoa almonds, chopped
- 1 tablespoon of ground coffee beans

HHHHHHHHHHHHHHHHHHHHHHHHHHHHHHH

Instructions:

1. Add a sheet of aluminum foil into a baking dish. Grease with cooking spray.

2. In a saucepan set over medium heat, add in the condensed milk. Allow to come to a simmer. Add in the milk chocolate. Cook for 1 to 2 minutes or until melted.

3. Add in the ground coffee beans and 1 cup of chopped cocoa almonds. Stir well to mix.

4. Pour into the baking dish.

5. Top off with the remaining chopped cocoa almonds.

6. Cover and place into the fridge to chill for 1 hour.

7. Slice and serve.

Recipe 6: Orange Creamsicle Fudge

This is one delicious fudge recipe that even the pickiest of eaters won't be able to resist once they get a taste of it themselves.

Yield: 16 servings

Preparation Time: 2 to 3 hours and 10 minutes

List of Ingredients:

- 1, 12-ounce bag of white chocolate chips
- 1, 16-ounce tub of vanilla frosting
- ½ teaspoons of orange extract
- 2 to 3 drops of orange food coloring

HHHHHHHHHHHHHHHHHHHHHHHHHHHHHHHH

Instructions:

1. Add a sheet of aluminum foil into a baking dish. Grease with cooking spray.

2. In a bowl, add in the white chocolate chips. Microwave for 1 to 2 minutes or until melted. Add in the tub of vanilla frosting. Microwave for an additional 30 seconds.

3. Pour ½ of this mix into a separate bowl. In one bowl, add in the orange extract and drops of orange food coloring. Stir well to mix. Add the remaining fudge mix. Stir well to mix.

4. Pour into the baking dish.

5. Cover and place into the fridge to chill for 2 to 3 hours.

6. Slice and serve.

Recipe 7: Dark Chocolate Bourbon Fudge

This is a simple and delicious fudge recipe that can be made in just a matter of minutes. It is made with plenty of chocolate to satisfy every chocoholic.

Yield: 8 servings

Preparation Time: 1 hour and 5 minutes

List of Ingredients:

- 2 ½ cups of white sugar
- 8 Tablespoons of butter
- ½ cup of whole milk
- ½ teaspoons of pure vanilla
- 13 marshmallows, cut in half
- 1 cup of Ghiradelli chocolate chips
- 1 ¼ cup of powdered sugar
- ¼ cup + 2 Tablespoons of bourbon
- ¼ teaspoons of fleur de sel

HHHHHHHHHHHHHHHHHHHHHHHHHHHHHHH

Instructions:

1. Place a sheet of aluminum foil into a baking dish. Grease with cooking spray.

2. In a bowl, add in the powdered sugar and bourbon. Stir well to mix. Set this mix aside.

3. In a pot set over medium to high heat, add in the white sugar, butter and whole milk. Stir to mix and allow to come to a boil. Cook for 3 minutes. Remove from heat. Add in the pure vanilla, marshmallow halves and chocolate chips. Stir well until melted.

4. Add in the bourbon mix and stir until evenly blended.

5. Pour into the baking dish.

6. Sprinkle the fleur de sel over the top.

7. Cover and place into the fridge to chill for 1 hour or until firm.

8. Slice and serve.

Recipe 8: Key Lime Fudge

This is an easy fudge recipe you can make if you love the flavor of traditional key lime pie. It is full of a fresh lime flavor I know you will love.

Yield: 8 servings

Preparation Time: 1 hour and 5 minutes

List of Ingredients:

- ¼ cup of butter, melted
- ¼ cup of white sugar
- 1, 9-piece pack of graham crackers
- 2, 11-ounce bags of white chocolate chips
- 1, 14 ounce can of sweetened condensed milk
- 2 Tablespoons of grated lime zest
- 3 Tablespoons of lime juice

HHHHHHHHHHHHHHHHHHHHHHHHHHHHHHH

Instructions:

1. Preheat the oven to 375 degrees. Add a sheet of aluminum foil into a baking dish. Grease with cooking spray.

2. In a food processor, add in the graham crackers. Pulse until crumbly in consistency. Transfer into a bowl.

3. In the bowl, add in the melted butter and white sugar. Stir well to mix. Press into the baking dish.

4. Place into the oven to bake for 5 to 8 minutes or until browned around the edges. Remove and set aside to cool completely.

5. In a bowl, add in the white chocolate chips and condensed milk. Microwave for 30 seconds or until the chocolate chips are melted. Stir well until smooth in consistency. Add in the grated lime zest and lime juice. Stir well to incorporate.

6. Pour over the crust.

7. Cover and place into the fridge to chill for 2 to 3 hours.

8. Slice and serve.

Recipe 9: Cookie Butter Pecan Fudge

This is a fudge that only needs three simple ingredients to put together, making it one of the easiest fudge recipes you can prepare.

Yield: 12 servings

Preparation Time: 3 hours and 10 minutes

List of Ingredients:

- 1, 14-ounce tub of vanilla frosting
- 1 ½ cups of cookie butter
- ½ cup of pecans, cut into halves

HHHHHHHHHHHHHHHHHHHHHHHHHHHHHHH

Instructions:

1. In a baking dish, add a sheet of parchment paper.

2. In a bowl, add in the cookie butter and vanilla frosting. Microwave for 1 minute. Stir until smooth in consistency. Add in the pecan halves and stir well to incorporate.

3. Pour into the baking dish.

4. Cover and place into the fridge to chill for 2 to 3 hours or until firm.

5. Slice and serve.

Recipe 10: Mint Chocolate Chip Fudge

If you love the flavor of mint chocolate chip ice cream, then this is one fudge dish I know you won't be able to help but fall in love with.

Yield: 12 servings

Preparation Time: 2 hours and 10 minutes

List of Ingredients:

- 3 ¼ cups of white chocolate chips
- 2 Tablespoons of butter
- 1, 14 ounce can of sweetened condensed milk
- 2 to 3 teaspoons of mint extract
- 3 drops of green food coloring
- ¾ cups of miniature chocolate chips, evenly divided

HHHHHHHHHHHHHHHHHHHHHHHHHHHHHH

Instructions:

1. Add a sheet of aluminum foil into a baking dish. Grease with cooking spray.

2. In a bowl, add in the white chocolate chips and butter. Microwave for 1 minute. Stir well until smooth in consistency. Add in the condensed milk and mint extract.

3. Add in the drops of green food coloring and ½ cup of miniature chocolate chips. Fold to gently incorporate.

4. Pour into the baking dish.

5. Sprinkle the remaining miniature chocolate chips over the top.

6. Cover and place into the fridge to chill for 2 hours.

7. Slice and serve.

Recipe 11: Rocky Road Fudge

This is a tasty fudge recipe that will remind you of the rocky road ice cream you have come to fall in love with.

Yield: 8 servings

Preparation Time: 1 hour and 5 minutes

List of Ingredients:

- 2 Tablespoons + 1 tablespoon of butter, evenly divided
- 1, 14 ounce can of sweetened condensed milk
- 2 cups of semi-sweet chocolate chips
- 1 teaspoon of pure vanilla
- 1 cup of peanuts, chopped
- 2 to 3 cups of marshmallows

HHHHHHHHHHHHHHHHHHHHHHHHHHHHHHHH

Instructions:

1. Place a sheet of aluminum foil into a baking dish. Grease with 1 tablespoon of butter.

2. In a saucepan set over medium heat, add in the remaining butter and can of condensed milk. Add in the semi-sweet chocolate chips. Cook for 2 to 3 minutes or until melted.

3. Remove from heat. Add in the pure vanilla. Stir well to mix.

4. Add in the chopped peanuts and marshmallows. Fold gently to incorporate.

5. Pour into the baking dish.

6. Cover and place into the fridge to chill for 1 hour.

7. Slice and serve.

Recipe 12: Snickerdoodle Fudge

This is a delicious way to turn your favorite cookie into a fudge recipe that everybody will fall in love with once they try it.

Yield: 64 servings

Preparation Time: 1 hour and 10 minutes

List of Ingredients:

- 1, 12-ounce bag of white chocolate chips
- 1, 16-ounce container of cream cheese frosting
- 2 teaspoons of cream of tartar
- ¼ cup of white sugar
- 2 teaspoons of powdered cinnamon

HHHHHHHHHHHHHHHHHHHHHHHHHHHHHHH

Instructions:

1. In a baking dish, add in a sheet of aluminum foil. Grease with cooking spray.

2. In a bowl, add in the white chocolate chips.

3. Add the cream cheese frosting in a separate bowl. Microwave for 20 to 30 minutes or until melted. Add in the cream of tartar and stir well to mix. Pour ¾ of this cream cheese over the white chocolate chips.

4. Add in the powdered cinnamon into the remaining cream cheese mix. Stir well until incorporated.

5. Pour half of the mix into the baking dish. Top off with the remaining cream cheese mix.

6. Cover and place into the fridge to chill for 1 hour.

7. Slice and serve.

Recipe 13: Gingerbread Fudge

This is a great tasting fudge dish you can make just in time for the holiday season. One bite of this fudge and you will become hooked.

Yield: 8 servings

Preparation Time: 1 hour and 5 minutes

List of Ingredients:

- 3 ¼ cups of white chocolate chips
- ½ cup of light brown sugar
- ½ cup of molasses
- 1/3 cup of evaporated milk
- 1 teaspoon of powdered cinnamon
- ½ teaspoons of powdered ginger
- ½ teaspoons of allspice
- ½ teaspoons of powdered nutmeg
- ½ teaspoons of powdered cloves
- 1 teaspoon of pure vanilla
- Green, white and green sprinkles, for topping

HHHHHHHHHHHHHHHHHHHHHHHHHHHHHH

Instructions:

1. Place a sheet of aluminum foil into a baking dish. Grease with cooking spray.

2. In a saucepan set over medium heat, add in the white chocolate chips, light brown sugar, molasses, evaporated milk, powdered cinnamon, powdered ginger, allspice, powdered nutmeg, powdered cloves and pure vanilla. Stir well until evenly blended. Cook for 3 minutes or until smooth in consistency.

3. Pour into the baking dish.

4. Sprinkle the sprinkles over the top.

5. Cover and place into the fridge to chill for 1 hour.

6. Slice and serve.

Recipe 14: Peanut Butter Snickers Fudge

This is a great tasting fudge you can make whenever you are craving your favorite chocolate bars. It only requires a few ingredients to prepare, making it perfect for those who need something simple to make.

Yield: 50 servings

Preparation Time: 3 hours and 10 minutes

List of Ingredients:

- 1, 14 ounce can of sweetened condensed milk
- 1 cup of white chocolate chips
- 1 ½ cup of peanut butter chips
- ¼ cup of creamy peanut butter
- 14 small snicker bars, chopped

HHHHHHHHHHHHHHHHHHHHHHHHHHHHHH

Instructions:

1. In a bowl, add in the white chocolate chips, peanut butter chips and creamy peanut butter. Stir well to mix.

2. In a saucepan set over medium heat, add in the sweetened milk. Cook for 3 minutes or until simmering. Remove from heat and pour over the chocolate chips. Stir well until melted.

3. Add in 2/3 of the chopped snickers bars.

4. Spread into an aluminum foil lined baking dish.

5. Sprinkle the remaining chopped snicker bars over the top.

6. Cover and place into the fridge to chill for 3 hours.

7. Slice and serve.

Recipe 15: German Chocolate Fudge

This is a fudge dish that every chocolate lover is going to fall in love with. Topped off with a coconut icing, this is one fudge dish that is perfect to make during every occasion.

Yield: 50 servings

Preparation Time: 1 hour and 12 minutes

List of Ingredients:

- 3 cups of milk chocolate chips
- 2 Tablespoons of butter
- 1, 14 ounce can of sweetened condensed milk
- 1, 3.9-ounce box of chocolate pudding mix
- 1, 7-ounce jar of marshmallow cream
- 1, 15.5 ounce can of coconut pecan frosting

HHHHHHHHHHHHHHHHHHHHHHHHHHHHHHH

Instructions:

1. In a baking dish, add a sheet of aluminum foil. Grease with cooking spray.

2. In a saucepan set over medium heat, add in the milk chocolate chips, 2 tablespoons of butter and condensed milk. Cook for 1 minute or until melted.

3. Add in the chocolate pudding mix. Continue to cook for an additional 1 to 2 minutes.

4. Add in the marshmallow cream. Stir well to mix. Remove from heat.

5. Pour into the baking dish.

6. Cover and place into the fridge to chill for 1 hour.

7. Spread the coconut pecan icing over the top.

8. Slice and serve.

Recipe 16: Cookie Monster Fudge

Just as the name implies, this is one fudge recipe that even the cookie monster will be envious of. It is a fudge dish that is loaded with chocolate chip and Oreo cookies, making this one fudge dish that every picky child will love.

Yield: 12 servings

Preparation Time: 3 to 4 hours and 10 minutes

List of Ingredients:

- 3 cups of blue candy melts
- 1, 14 ounce can of sweetened condensed milk
- ½ cup of miniature Oreos, extra for topping
- ½ cup of chocolate chip cookies, broken and extra for topping

HHHHHHHHHHHHHHHHHHHHHHHHHHHHHHH

Instructions:

1. Add a sheet of aluminum foil into a baking dish. Grease with cooking spray.

2. In a saucepan set over low heat, add in the blue candy melts and sweetened milk. Cook for 1 to 2 minutes or until melted. Add in the miniature Oreos and chocolate chip cookies. Stir well to incorporate. Remove from heat.

3. Pour into the baking dish.

4. Sprinkle the extra miniature Oreos and chocolate chip cookies over the top.

5. Cover and place into the fridge to chill for 3 to 4 hours.

6. Slice and serve.

Recipe 17: Sugar Cookie Fudge

This is the perfect fudge dish to make whenever you are craving something on the sweeter side. This is easy to make and contains all of the flavor of homemade sugar cookies that you love.

Yield: 24 servings

Preparation Time: 1 hour and 5 minutes

List of Ingredients:

- 2 cups of sugar cookie mix
- 2 cups of powdered sugar
- ¼ cup of sugar cookie creamer
- ½ cup of butter
- 2/3 cup of white chocolate chips
- 1 teaspoon of pure vanilla
- ½ cup of rainbow sprinkles, for topping

HHHHHHHHHHHHHHHHHHHHHHHHHHHHHHH

Instructions:

1. Place a sheet of aluminum foil into a baking dish. Grease with cooking spray.

2. In a bowl, add in the sugar cookie mix and powdered sugar. Stir well to mix. Add in the butter and cut in with a pastry cutter until crumbly in consistency. Add in the sugar cookie creamer.

3. Place into the microwave and cook for 2 minutes on the highest setting. Stir well. Add in the white chocolate chips and pure vanilla. Stir well until smooth in consistency.

4. Pour into the baking dish.

5. Sprinkle the rainbow sprinkles over the top.

6. Cover and place into the fridge to chill for 1 hour.

7. Slice and serve.

Recipe 18: Root Beer Fudge

This is a fudge dish you can make whenever you need to spoil yourself during the summer season. It is so tasty, even the pickiest of eaters won't be able to turn this fudge down.

Yield: 8 servings

Preparation Time: 1 hour and 5 minutes

List of Ingredients:

- 1 teaspoon + ¾ cup of butter, evenly divided
- 3 cups of white sugar
- 1, 5 ounce can of evaporated milk
- 10 to 12 ounces of white chocolate baking chips
- 7 ounces of marshmallow crème
- ½ teaspoons of pure vanilla
- 2 teaspoons of concentrated root beer

HHHHHHHHHHHHHHHHHHHHHHHHHHHHHH

Instructions:

1. Add a sheet of aluminum foil into a baking dish. Grease with 1 teaspoon of butter.

2. In a saucepan set over medium heat, add in the white sugar, evaporated milk and ¾ cup of butter. Allow to come to a boil. Cook for 4 minutes. Remove from heat and stir well to mix.

3. Add in the white chocolate chips and marshmallow crème. Stir well until melted.

4. Place 1/3 of the white chocolate mix aside. In the remaining mix, add in the pure vanilla. Stir well to mix. In the reserved white chocolate mix, add in the concentrated root beer. Stir well to incorporate.

5. Spread the root beer mix into the baking dish. Spread the remaining white chocolate mix over the top.

6. Cover and place into the fridge to chill for 1 hour.

7. Slice and serve.

Recipe 19: Caramel Apple Fudge

This is the perfect fudge recipe to make just in time for Thanksgiving. It is elegant enough to serve during your next Thanksgiving feast.

Yield: 8 servings

Preparation Time: 2 hours and 10 minutes

List of Ingredients:

- 1, 12-ounce bag of white chocolate chips
- 1, 16-ounce tub of caramel apple frosting
- 2 Tablespoons of butter
- 1, 15-ounce bag of dried apples, chopped

HHHHHHHHHHHHHHHHHHHHHHHHHHHHHHHH

Instructions:

1. Add a sheet of aluminum foil into a baking dish. Grease with cooking spray.

2. In a bowl, add in the white chocolate chips, caramel and apple frosting and butter. Microwave for 1 minute. Stir well until smooth in consistency.

3. Add in the dried chopped apples. Stir well to incorporate.

4. Pour into the baking dish.

5. Cover and place into the fridge to chill for 2 hours.

6. Slice and serve.

Recipe 20: Cake Batter Fudge

This is the perfect fudge dish to make whenever you have a strong sweet tooth that needs to be satisfied. It is rich, smooth and absolutely delicious.

Yield: 12 servings

Preparation Time: 1 hour and 10 minutes

List of Ingredients:

- 2 ½ cup of vanilla cake mix
- 2 cups of powdered sugar
- 2/3 cup of butter, cut into pieces
- ¼ cup of whole milk
- ¾ cup of white chocolate chips
- ½ cup of rainbow sprinkles, plus extra for topping

HHHHHHHHHHHHHHHHHHHHHHHHHHHHHHH

Instructions:

1. In a bowl, add in the vanilla cake mix and powdered sugar. Stir well to mix.

2. Add in the butter pieces and whole milk. Place into the microwave and cook for 1 to 2 minutes or until melted. Stir well to mix.

3. Add the white chocolate chips into a separate bowl. Melt in the microwave for 30 seconds. Pour into the cake mix. Stir well to mix. Add in the sprinkles and fold to incorporate.

4. Pour into a greased and aluminum foil lined baking dish. Sprinkle extra rainbow sprinkles over the top.

5. Cover and place into the fridge to chill for 1 hour.

6. Slice and serve.

Recipe 21: White Chocolate Peppermint Fudge

This is a creamy chocolate fudge recipe mixed with the perfect amount of peppermint that will be a welcome treat during Christmas.

Yield: 64 servings

Preparation Time: 1 hour and 5 minutes

List of Ingredients:

- 2 ½ cups of white chocolate chips
- 1, 14 ounce can of sweetened condensed milk
- 1 teaspoon of peppermint extract
- 1 cup of peppermint baking chips
- ½ cup of peppermint candies, crushed

HHHHHHHHHHHHHHHHHHHHHHHHHHHHHHH

Instructions:

1. In a baking dish, add a sheet of aluminum foil. Grease with cooking spray.

2. In a double boiler set over medium heat, add in the white chocolate chips and condensed milk. Cook for 1 to 3 minutes or until melted. Remove from heat. Add in the peppermint extract and peppermint baking chips. Stir well until melted.

3. Pour into the baking dish.

4. Sprinkle the crushed peppermint candies over the top.

5. Cover and place into the fridge to chill for 1 hour.

6. Slice and serve.

Recipe 22: Carrot Cake Fudge

If you love the flavor of a traditional carrot cake, then this is one fudge dish I know you are going to want to make as often as possible.

Yield: 12 servings

Preparation Time: 1 hour and 10 minutes

List of Ingredients:

- 4 cups of white chocolate chips
- 1 cup of sweetened condensed milk
- 2 ½ Tablespoons of carrot baby food
- ½ teaspoons of powdered cinnamon
- ¼ teaspoons of powdered nutmeg

Instructions:

1. Add a sheet of aluminum foil into a baking dish. Grease with cooking spray.

2. In a saucepan set over medium heat, add in the white chocolate chips and the condensed milk. Cook for 1 to 2 minutes or until smooth in consistency.

3. Add in the carrot baby food, powdered cinnamon and powdered nutmeg. Stir well until incorporated.

4. Pour into the baking dish.

5. Cover and place into the fridge to chill for 1 hour.

6. Slice and serve.

Recipe 23: Hazelnut and Chocolate Pirouline Fudge

This is a classic holiday twist on a typical fudge recipe that the entire family will fall in love with. Since it is made in the microwave, it is one of the easiest fudge recipes you can prepare.

Yield: 36 servings

Preparation Time: 1 hour and 10 minutes

List of Ingredients:

- 1 cup of butter, extra for greasing
- 1 cup of chocolate and hazelnut spread
- 1 teaspoon of pure vanilla
- 1 pound of powdered sugar
- 22 Pirouline rolled wafers

HHHHHHHHHHHHHHHHHHHHHHHHHHHHHH

Instructions:

1. Add a sheet of aluminum foil into a baking dish. Grease with butter.

2. In a bowl, add in 1 cup of butter and the chocolate and hazelnut spread. Cover and place into the microwave to cook for 2 minutes. Remove and stir gently. Continue to microwave for an additional 2 minutes.

3. Add in the pure vanilla and powdered sugar. Stir well until incorporated.

4. Pour half into the baking dish.

5. Add a layer of the wafers. Pour the remaining chocolate mix over the top.

6. Cover and place into the fridge to chill for 1 hour.

7. Slice and serve.

Recipe 24: Nutter Butter Fudge

This is a hearty and delicious fudge recipe you can make that is packed full of a chocolatey flavor that is impossible to resist.

Yield: 8 servings

Preparation Time: 1 hour and 5 minutes

List of Ingredients:

- 8 Tablespoons of butter, soft
- 4 cups of white chocolate chips
- 1 cup of sweetened condensed milk
- 1, 7-ounce container of marshmallow crème
- 20 nutter butter cookies, crushed
- 4 nutter butter cookies, for topping

HHHHHHHHHHHHHHHHHHHHHHHHHHHHHHHH

Instructions:

1. In a baking dish, add a sheet of aluminum foil. Grease with cooking spray.

2. In a saucepan set over medium heat, add in the butter. Once melted, add in the condensed milk and white chocolate chips. Cook for 3 minutes or until melted. Add in the marshmallow crème. Remove from heat.

3. Add in the crushed nutter butter cookies. Fold to incorporate.

4. Spread into the baking dish.

5. Top off with the remaining nutter butter cookies.

6. Cover and place into the fridge to chill for 1 hour.

7. Slice and serve.

Recipe 25: S'mores Fudge

With the help of this delicious fudge recipe, you won't have to go camping in order to enjoy homemade s'mores.

Yield: 24 servings

Preparation Time: 35 minutes

Ingredients for the crust:

- 4 sheets of graham crackers, crushed
- ¼ cup of white sugar
- 1 ½ Tablespoons of butter, melted

Ingredients for the fudge:

- 1 ½ cups of milk chocolate chips
- ½ teaspoons of pure vanilla
- ½, 14 ounce can of sweetened condensed milk

Ingredients for the marshmallow:

- 1 cup of chocolate chips
- ½ cup of marshmallow fluff
- ½, 14 ounce can of sweetened condensed milk

HHHHHHHHHHHHHHHHHHHHHHHHHHHHHH

Instructions:

1. Preheat the oven to 375 degrees. In a baking dish, add a sheet of aluminum foil. Grease with cooking spray.

2. In a bowl, add in the crushed graham crackers, melted butter and white sugar. Stir well until evenly mixed. Press into the baking dish.

3. Place into the oven to bake for 15 minutes or until golden around the edges.

4. In a saucepan set over low heat, add in the milk chocolate chips and sweetened milk. Add in the pure vanilla. Cook for 3 minutes or until melted. Pour into the baking dish.

5. In a separate saucepan set over low heat, add in the white chocolate chips. Add in the marshmallow fluffy and condensed milk. Cook for 3 minutes or until smooth in consistency. Pour over the chocolate layer.

6. Cover and place into the fridge to chill for 1 hour.

7. Slice and serve.

About the Author

Angel Burns learned to cook when she worked in the local seafood restaurant near her home in Hyannis Port in Massachusetts as a teenager. The head chef took Angel under his wing and taught the young woman the tricks of the trade for cooking seafood. The skills she had learned at a young age helped her get accepted into Boston University's Culinary Program where she also minored in business administration.

Summers off from school meant working at the same restaurant but when Angel's mentor and friend retired as head chef, she took over after graduation and created classic and new dishes that delighted the diners. The restaurant flourished under Angel's culinary creativity and one customer developed more than an appreciation for Angel's food. Several months after taking over the position, the young woman met her future husband at work and they have been inseparable ever since. They still live in Hyannis Port with their two children and a cocker spaniel named Buddy.

Angel Burns turned her passion for cooking and her business acumen into a thriving e-book business. She has authored several successful books on cooking different types of dishes using simple ingredients for novices and experienced chefs alike. She is still head chef in Hyannis Port and says she will probably never leave!

Author's Afterthoughts

With so many books out there to choose from, I want to thank you for choosing this one and taking precious time out of your life to buy and read my work. Readers like you are the reason I take such passion in creating these books.

It is with gratitude and humility that I express how honored I am to become a part of your life and I hope that you take the same pleasure in reading this book as I did in writing it.

Can I ask one small favour? I ask that you write an honest and open review on Amazon of what you thought of the book. This will help other readers make an informed choice on whether to buy this book.

My sincerest thanks,

Angel Burns

If you want to be the first to know about news, new books, events and giveaways, subscribe to my newsletter by clicking the link below

https://angel-burns.gr8.com

or Scan QR-code

Printed in Great Britain
by Amazon